6 Full-Length SBAC Grade 5 Math Practice Tests

Extra Test Prep to Help Ace the SBAC Grade 5 Math Test

By

Michael Smith & Reza Nazari

6 Full-Length SBAC Grade 5 Math Practice Tests

Published in the United State of America By

The Math Notion

Web: WWW.MathNotion.Com

Email: info@Mathnotion.com

About the Author

Michael Smith has been a math instructor for over a decade now. He holds a master's degree in Management. Since 2006, Michael has devoted his time to both teaching and developing exceptional math learning materials. As a Math instructor and test prep expert, Michael has worked with thousands of students. He has used the feedback of his students to develop a unique study program that can be used by students to drastically improve their math score fast and effectively.

– SAT Math Practice Book

– ACT Math Practice Book

– GRE Math Practice Book

– Common Core Math Practice Book

–many Math Education Workbooks, Exercise Books and Study Guides

As an experienced Math teacher, Mr. Smith employs a variety of formats to help students achieve their goals: He tutors online and in person, he teaches students in large groups, and he provides training materials and textbooks through his website and through Amazon.

You can contact Michael via email at:

info@Mathnotion.com

Prepare for the SBAC Grade 5 Math test with a perfect practice book!

The surest way to practice your SBAC Math test-taking skills is with simulated exams. This comprehensive practice book with 6 full length and realistic SBAC Math practice tests help you measure your exam readiness, find your weak areas, and succeed on the SBAC Math test. The detailed answers and explanations for each SBAC Math question help you master every aspect of the SBAC Math.

6 Full-length SBAC Grade 5 Math Practice Tests is a prestigious resource to help you succeed on the SBAC Math test. This perfect practice book features:

- Content 100% aligned with the SBAC test
- Six full-length SBAC Math practice tests similar to the actual test in length, format, question types, and degree of difficulty
- Detailed answers and explanations for the SBAC Math practice questions
- Written by SBAC Math top instructors and experts

After completing this hands-on exercise book, you will gain confidence, strong foundation, and adequate practice to succeed on the SBAC Math test.

WWW.MathNotion.COM

… So Much More Online!

✓ FREE Math Lessons

✓ More Math Learning Books!

✓ Mathematics Worksheets

✓ Online Math Tutors

For a PDF Version of This Book

Please Visit WWW.MathNotion.com

Contents

SBAC Math Practice Tests

Smarter Balanced Assessment Consortium (SBAC) test assesses student mastery of the common core State Standards.

The SBAC is a computer adaptive test. It means that there is a set of test questions in a variety of question types that adjust to each student based on the student's answers to previous questions. This section includes a range of items types, such as selecting several correct responses for one item, typing out a response, fill---in short answers/tables, graphing, drag and drop, etc.

On computer adaptive tests, if the correct answer is chosen, the next question will be harder. If the answer given is incorrect, the next question will be easier. This also means that once an answer is selected on the computer it cannot be changed.

In this section, there are 2 complete SBAC Math Tests that reflect the format and question types on SBAC. On a real SBAC Math test, the number of questions varies and there are about 30 questions.

Let your student take these tests to see what score he or she will be able to receive on a real SBAC test.

Time to Test

Time to refine your skill with a practice examination

Take a REAL SBAC Mathematics test to simulate the test day experience. After you've finished, score your test using the answer key.

Before You Start

- You'll need a pencil and scratch papers to take the test.
- For this practice test, don't time yourself. Spend time as much as you need.
- It's okay to guess. You won't lose any points if you're wrong.
- After you've finished the test, review the answer key to see where you went wrong.

Calculators are not permitted for Grade 5 SBAC Tests

Good Luck!

SBAC GRADE 5 MAHEMATICS REFRENCE MATERIALS

Perimeter

Square $P = 4S$

Rectangle $P = 2L + 2W$

Area

Square $A = S \times S$

Rectangle $A = l \times w$ or $A = bh$

Volume

Square $A = S \times S \times S$

Rectangle $A = l \times w \times h$ or $A = Bh$

LENGTH

Customary	Metric
1 mile (mi) = 1,760 yards (yd)	1 kilometer (km) = 1,000 meters (m)
1 yard (yd) = 3 feet (ft)	1 meter (m) = 100 centimeters (cm)
1 foot (ft) = 12 inches (in.)	1 centimeter (cm) = 10 millimeters (mm)

VOLUME AND CAPACITY

Customary	Metric
1 gallon (gal) = 4 quarts (qt)	1 liter (L) = 1,000 milliliters (mL)
1 quart (qt) = 2 pints (pt.)	
1 pint (pt.) = 2 cups (c)	
1 cup (c) = 8 fluid ounces (Fl oz)	

WEIGHT AND MASS

Customary	Metric
1 ton (T) = 2,000 pounds (lb.)	1 kilogram (kg) = 1,000 grams (g)
1 pound (lb.) = 16 ounces (oz)	1 gram (g) = 1,000 milligrams (mg)

Smarter Balanced Assessment Consortium

Practice Test 1

Mathematics

GRADE 5

❖ **30 questions**

❖ **There is no time limit for this practice test.**

❖ **Calculators are NOT permitted for this practice test**

Administered Month Year

1) The drivers at G & G trucking must report the mileage on their trucks each week. The mileage reading of Ed's vehicle was 43,907 at the beginning of one week, and 44,053 at the end of the same week. What was the total number of miles driven by Ed that week?

A. 46 MILES

B. 145 MILES

C. 146 MILES

D. 1,046 MILES

2) Camille uses a 40% off coupon when buying a sweater that costs $30. How much does she pay?

A. $18

B. $25

C. $40.50

D. $43

3) The area of a rectangle is D square feet and its length is 7 feet. Which equation represents W, the width of the rectangle in feet?

A. $W = \dfrac{D}{7}$

B. $W = \dfrac{7}{D}$

C. $W = 7D$

D. $W = 7 + D$

4) A baker uses 3 eggs to bake a cake. How many cakes will he be able to bake with 210 eggs?

   A. 65

   B. 70

   C. 56

   D. 45

5) Which list shows the fractions in order from least to greatest?

$$\frac{3}{4}, \frac{6}{7}, \frac{2}{10}, \frac{1}{2}, \frac{6}{14}$$

   A. $\frac{3}{4}, \frac{6}{7}, \frac{2}{10}, \frac{1}{2}, \frac{6}{14}$

   B. $\frac{6}{14}, \frac{1}{2}, \frac{3}{4}, \frac{6}{7}, \frac{2}{10}$

   C. $\frac{2}{10}, \frac{3}{4}, \frac{6}{7}, \frac{1}{2}, \frac{6}{14}$

   D. $\frac{2}{10}, \frac{6}{14}, \frac{1}{2}, \frac{3}{4}, \frac{6}{7}$

6) Which statement about 5 multiplied by $\frac{4}{3}$ is true?

   A. The product is between 3 and 4

   B. The product is between 6 and 7

   C. The product is more than $\frac{11}{3}$

   D. The product is between $\frac{14}{3}$ and 5

7) A shirt costing $150 is discounted 10%. Which of the following expressions can be used to find the selling price of the shirt?

    A. (150) (0.70)

    B. (150) – 150 (0.30)

    C. (150) (0.15) – (150) (0.15)

    D. (150) (0.9)

8) Which of the following angles is obtuse?

    A. 30 Degrees

    B. 45 Degrees

    C. 80 Degrees

    D. 120 Degrees

9) If A = 30, then which of the following equations are correct?

    A. A + 30 = 60

    B. A ÷ 30 = 60

    C. 30 × A = 60

    D. A – 30 = 60

10) The perimeter of the trapezoid below is 50. What is its area?

    A. 352

    B. 132

    C. 110

    D. 50

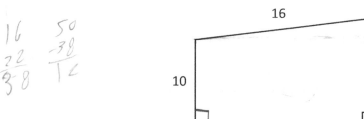

11) In a bag, there are 40 cards. Of these cards, 8 cards are white. What fraction of

the cards are white?

A. $\frac{1}{5}$

B. $\frac{4}{10}$

C. $\frac{32}{40}$

D. $\frac{2}{20}$

12) A rope weighs 500 grams per meter of length. What is the weight in kilograms

of 12.2 meters of this rope? (1 kilograms = 1000 grams)

A. 0.061

B. 0.61

C. 6.1

D. 6,100

13) Lily and Ella are in a pancake–eating contest. Lily can eat three pancakes per

minute, while Ella can eat 2 ½ pancakes per minute. How many total pancakes

can they eat in 5 minutes?

A. 9.5 Pancakes

B. 29.5 Pancakes

C. 22.5 Pancakes

D. 27.5 Pancakes

14) How many $\frac{1}{4}$ cup servings are in a package of cheese that contains $5\frac{1}{2}$ cups altogether?

A. $\frac{11}{8}$

B. 22

C. 11

D. $\frac{8}{11}$

15) With what number must 5.253691 be multiplied in order to obtain the number 52,536.91?

A. 100

B. 1,000

C. 10,000

D. 100,000

16) What is the volume of this box?

A. 124 cm³

B. 86 cm³

C. 280 cm³

D. 315 cm³

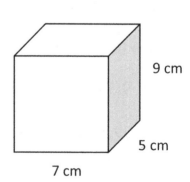

9 cm

5 cm

7 cm

17) 25 is What percent of 40?

   A. 20 %

   B. 62 %

   C. 62.5 %

   D. 150 %

18) The area of a circle is 36π. What is the circumference of the circle?

   A. 8 π

   B. 12 π

   C. 32 π

   D. 64 π

19) The distance between cities A and B is approximately 1,960 miles. If Alice drive an average of 56 miles per hour, how many hours will it take Alice to drive from city A to city B?

   A. Approximately 41 Hours

   B. Approximately 35 Hours

   C. Approximately 29 Hours

   D. Approximately 27 Hours

20) 10 yards 3 feet and 4 inches equals to how many inches?

   A. 96

   B. 432

   C. 400

   D. 578

21) Which expression has a value of – 7?

    A. $7 + (+3) + (-17)$

    B. $1 + (-3) \times (-2)$

    C. $-6 \times (-6) + (-2) \times (-12)$

    D. $(-2) \times (-7) + 4$

22) Solve.

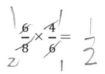

    A. $\dfrac{1}{2}$

    B. $\dfrac{10}{40}$

    C. $\dfrac{20}{60}$

    D. $\dfrac{1}{4}$

23) The length of a rectangle is $\dfrac{5}{6}$ of inches and the width of the rectangle is $\dfrac{2}{15}$ of inches. What is the area of that rectangle?

    A. $\dfrac{1}{2}$

    B. $\dfrac{1}{9}$

    C. $\dfrac{10}{45}$

    D. $\dfrac{12}{75}$

24) ABC Corporation earned only $300,000 during the previous year, three–second only of the management's predicted income. How much earning did the management predict?

  A. $30,000

  B. $20,000

  C. $200,000

  D. $240,000

25) How many square feet of tile is needed for 16 feet to 16 feet room?

  A. 85 Square Feet

  B. 120 Square Feet

  C. 216 Square Feet

  D. 256 Square Feet

26) Solve. $\frac{1}{2} + \frac{4}{7} - \frac{1}{14} =$

  A. $\frac{9}{10}$

  B. $\frac{2}{10}$

  C. 1

  D. 14

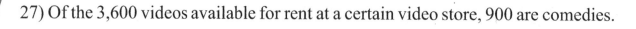

27) Of the 3,600 videos available for rent at a certain video store, 900 are comedies.

What percent of the videos are comedies?

A. 18 ½ %

B. 20%

C. 22%

D. 25%

28) How many 3 × 3 squares can fit inside a rectangle with a height of 52 and width

of 18?

A. 104

B. 85

C. 60

D. 88

29) William keeps track of the length of each fish that he catches. Following are

the lengths in inches of the fish that he caught one day: 15, 16, 9, 14, 9, 10, 18

What is the median fish length that William caught that day?

A. 18 Inches

B. 9 Inches

C. 10 Inches

D. 14 Inches

30) $6 + [6 \times 5] \div 2 = ?$

    A. 18

    B. 21

    C. 30

    D. 9

"This is the end of Practice Test 1"

Smarter Balanced Assessment Consortium

Practice Test 2

Mathematics

GRADE 5

- ❖ **30 questions**
- ❖ **There is no time limit for this practice test.**
- ❖ **Calculators are NOT permitted for this practice test**

Administered Month Year

1) Jack added 16 to the product of 14 and 22. What is this sum?

   A. 86

   B. 336

   C. 324

   D. 7,602

2) Joe makes $4.75 per hour at his work. If he works 6 hours, how much money will he earn?

   A. $33.00

   B. $32.75

   C. $36.50

   D. $28.5

3) What is the value of $5 - 3\frac{2}{9}$?

   A. $\frac{23}{9}$

   B. $1\frac{7}{9}$

   C. $-\frac{1}{9}$

   D. $\frac{42}{9}$

4) The bride and groom invited 230 guests for their wedding. 190 guests arrived.

What percent of the guest list was not present?

A. 70%

B. 40%

C. 43.32%

D. 17.4%

5) Frank wants to compare these two measurements.

19.023 kg ☐ 19,023 g

Which symbol should he use?

A. <

B. >

C. ≠

D. =

6) Aria was hired to teach three identical 5th grade math courses, which entailed being present in the classroom 24 hours altogether. At $20 per class hour, how much did Aria earn for teaching one course?

A. $50

B. $160

C. $300

D. $1,400

7) In a classroom of 50 students, 25 are male. What percentage of the class is female?

A. 25%

B. 40%

C. 50%

D. 75%

8) In a party, 8 soft drinks are required for every 12 guests. If there are 156 guests, how many soft drinks are required?

A. 18

B. 36

C. 104

D. 171

9) You are asked to chart the temperature during an 8–hour period to give the average. These are your results:

7 am: 3 degrees	11 am: 31 degrees
8 am: 6 degrees	12 pm: 34 degrees
9 am: 23 degrees	1 pm: 34 degrees
10 am: 29 degrees	2 pm: 32 degrees

What is the average temperature?

A. 24

B. 28

C. 36

D. 46

10) While at work, Emma checks her email once every 90 minutes. In 5 hours, how many times does she check her email?

A. 9 Times

B. 8 Times

C. 6 Times

D. 7 Times

11) In a classroom of 66 students, 30 are male. About what percentage of the class is female?

A. 53%

B. 54%

C. 55%

D. 56%

12) A florist has 585 flowers. How many full bouquets of 13 flowers can he make?

A. 40

B. 41

C. 43

D. 45

13) What is 6,123.48245 rounded to the nearest tenth?

A. 6,123.482

B. 6,123.5

C. 6,123

D. 6,123.48

14) If a rectangular swimming pool has a perimeter of 124 feet and it is 24 feet wide, what is its area?

A.1,896 square feet

B.2,600 square feet

C.1,325 square feet

D.912 square feet

15) What is the volume of the following rectangle prism?

A.15 ft³

B.20 ft3

C.24 ft3

D.210 ft³

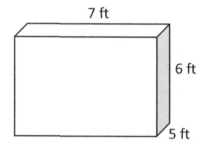

16) A circle has a diameter of 4 inches. What is its approximate circumference? (π = 3.14)

A. 6.23 inches

B. 12.56 inches

C. 32.65 inches

D. 36.12 inches

17) How long is the line segment shown on the number line below?

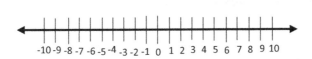

A. 10

B. 9

C. 8

D. 7

18) If $x = -2$, which equation is true?

A. $x(2x - 4) = 50$

B. $8(4 - x) = 48$

C. $2(4x + 6) = 10$

D. $6x - 2 = -23$

19) Peter traveled 160 miles in 4 hours and Jason traveled 240 miles in 8 hours.

What is the ratio of the average speed of Peter to average speed of Jason?

A. 4: 3

B. 2: 3

C. 5: 7

D. 5: 6

20) A woman owns a dog walking business. If 3 workers can walk 9 dogs, how many dogs can 6 workers walk?

   A. 12

   B. 18

   C. 16

   D. 19

21) Which list shows the fractions listed in order from least to greatest?

$$\frac{1}{3}, \frac{1}{10}, \frac{1}{6}, \frac{1}{8}$$

   A. $\frac{1}{8}, \frac{1}{3}, \frac{1}{10}, \frac{1}{6}$

   B. $\frac{1}{6}, \frac{1}{10}, \frac{1}{3}, \frac{1}{8}$

   C. $\frac{1}{3}, \frac{1}{6}, \frac{1}{8}, \frac{1}{10}$

   D. $\frac{1}{10}, \frac{1}{8}, \frac{1}{6}, \frac{1}{3}$

22) What are the coordinates of the intersection of $x-axis$ and the $y-axis$ on a coordinate plane?

   A. (5, 5)

   B. (1, 1)

   C. (0, 0)

   D. (0, 1)

23) In a triangle ABC the measure of angle ACB is 35° and the measure of angle CAB is 65°. What is the measure of angle ABC?

A. 100

B. 80

C. 55

D. 25

24) David's motorcycle stalled at the beach and he called the towing company. They charged him $ 3.75 per mile for the first 20 miles and then $4.15 per mile for each mile over 20. David was 28 miles from the motorcycle repair shop. How much was David's towing bill?

A. $105

B. $113

C. $108.20

D. $116.20

25) A car uses 15 gallons of gas to travel 675 miles. How many miles per gallon does the car get?

A. 26 miles per gallon

B. 28 miles per gallon

C. 45 miles per gallon

D. 35 miles per gallon

26) Five out of 35 students had to go to summer school. What is the ratio of students who did not have to go to summer school expressed, in its lowest terms?

A. $\frac{6}{7}$

B. $\frac{7}{8}$

C. $\frac{3}{4}$

D. $\frac{5}{7}$

27) A steak dinner at a restaurant costs $8.5. If a man buys a steak dinner for himself and 3 friends, what will the total cost be?

A. $42.50

B. $3400

C. $25.50

D. $17.00

28) If 4 garbage trucks can collect the trash of 32 homes in a day. How many trucks are needed to collect in 80 houses?

A. 8

B. 9

C. 5

D. 10

29) A barista averages making 12 cups of coffee per hour. At this rate, how many hours will it take until she's made 1080 cups of coffee?

A. 75

B. 90

C. 85

D. 90

30) Ava needs 1/5 of an ounce of salt to make 1 cup of dip for fries. How many cups of dip will she be able to make if she has 60 ounces of salt?

A. 45

B. 55

C. 75

D. 300

"This is the end of Practice Test 2"

Smarter Balanced Assessment Consortium

SBAC Practice Test 3

Mathematics

GRADE 5

- ❖ 30 Questions
- ❖ There is no time limit for this practice test.
- ❖ Calculators are NOT permitted for this practice test

Administered *Month Year*

1) The drivers at G & G trucking must report the mileage on their trucks each week. The mileage reading of Ed's vehicle was 44,476 at the beginning of one week, and 45,521 at the end of the same week. What was the total number of miles driven by Ed that week?

   A. 140 MILES

   B. 105 MILES

   C. 1,045 MILES

   D. 1,540 MILES

2) Camille uses a 20% off coupon when buying a sweater that costs $80. How much does she pay?

   A. $64

   B. $16

   C. $48

   D. $54

3) The area of a rectangle is D square feet and its length is 17 feet. Which equation represents W, the width of the rectangle in feet?

   A. $W = \dfrac{D}{17}$

   B. $W = \dfrac{17}{D}$

   C. $W = 17D$

   D. $W = 17 + D$

4) A baker uses 3 eggs to bake a cake. How many cakes will he be able to bake with 330 eggs?

A. 90

B. 110

C. 105

D. 95

5) Which list shows the fractions in order from least to greatest?

$$\frac{4}{5}, \frac{2}{5}, \frac{9}{10}, \frac{3}{8}, \frac{1}{6}$$

A. $\frac{4}{5}, \frac{2}{5}, \frac{9}{10}, \frac{1}{6}, \frac{3}{8}$

B. $\frac{3}{8}, \frac{1}{6}, \frac{4}{5}, \frac{2}{5}, \frac{9}{10}$

C. $\frac{9}{10}, \frac{4}{5}, \frac{2}{5}, \frac{1}{6}, \frac{3}{8}$

D. $\frac{1}{6}, \frac{3}{8}, \frac{2}{5}, \frac{4}{5}, \frac{9}{10}$

6) Which statement about 3 multiplied by $\frac{5}{4}$ is true?

A. The product is between 4 and 5

B. The product is between 3 and 4

C. The product is more than $\frac{19}{4}$

D. The product is between $\frac{11}{2}$ and 6

7) A shirt costing $150 is discounted 6%. Which of the following expressions can be used to find the selling price of the shirt?

   A. $(150)(0.06)$

   B. $(150) - 150(0.16)$

   C. $(150)(0.06) - (150)(0.60)$

   D. $(150)(0.94)$

8) Which of the following angles is acute?

   A. 100 Degrees

   B. 135 Degrees

   C. 170 Degrees

   D. 50 Degrees

9) If $A = 12$, then which of the following equations are correct?

   A. $A + 50 = 600$

   B. $A \div 50 = 600$

   C. $50 \times A = 600$

   D. $A - 50 = 600$

10) The perimeter of the trapezoid below is 40. What is its area?

   A. 94

   B. 98

   C. 96

   D. 86

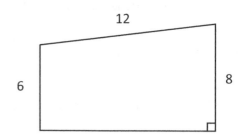

11) In a bag, there are 98 cards. Of these cards, 14 cards are white. What fraction of the cards are white?

A. $\frac{1}{7}$

B. $\frac{4}{7}$

C. $\frac{3}{14}$

D. $\frac{1}{19}$

12) A rope weighs 900 grams per meter of length. What is the weight in kilograms of 4.5 meters of this rope? (1 kilograms = 1000 grams)

A. 0.0405

B. 0.405

C. 4.05

D. 4,050

13) Lily and Ella are in a pancake–eating contest. Lily can eat three pancakes per minute, while Ella can eat $4\frac{1}{3}$ pancakes per minute. How many total pancakes can they eat in 9 minutes?

A. 69 Pancakes

B. 19 Pancakes

C. 39 Pancakes

D. 66 Pancakes

14) How many $\frac{1}{9}$ cup servings are in a package of cheese that contains $2\frac{1}{3}$ cups altogether?

  A. $\frac{7}{3}$

  B. 21

  C. 63

  D. $\frac{7}{9}$

15) With what number must 9.864589 be multiplied in order to obtain the number 986,458.9?

  A. 1,000

  B. 10,000

  C. 1,000,000

  D. 100,000

16) What is the volume of this box?

  A. 185 cm^3

  B. 85 cm^3

  C. 380 cm^3

  D. 385 cm^3

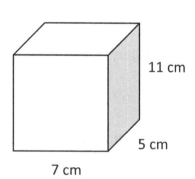

11 cm

5 cm

7 cm

17) 15 is What percent of 50?

    A. 70 %

    B. 60 %

    C. 30 %

    D. 130 %

18) The area of a circle is 121π. What is the circumference of the circle?

    A. $11\,\pi$

    B. $22\,\pi$

    C. $2421\,\pi$

    D. $44\,\pi$

19) The distance between cities A and B is approximately 1,960 miles. If Alice drive an average of 56 miles per hour, how many hours will it take Alice to drive from city A to city B?

    A. Approximately 38 Hours

    B. Approximately 35 Hours

    C. Approximately 23 Hours

    D. Approximately 47 Hours

20) 7 yards 6 feet and 18 inches equals to how many inches?

    A. 102

    B. 423

    C. 342

    D. 324

21) Which expression has a value of -13?

    A. $7 - (-5) + (-25)$

    B. $3 + (-3) \times (-9)$

    C. $-4 \times (-5) + (-2) \times (-10)$

    D. $(-7) \times (-4) + 2$

22) Solve. $\frac{5}{8} \times \frac{2}{5} =$

    A. $\frac{1}{4}$

    B. $\frac{1}{8}$

    C. $\frac{5}{8}$

    D. $\frac{1}{3}$

23) The length of a rectangle is $\frac{7}{10}$ of inches and the width of the rectangle is $\frac{5}{21}$ of inches. What is the area of that rectangle?

    A. $\frac{1}{10}$

    B. $\frac{1}{6}$

    C. $\frac{7}{16}$

    D. $\frac{35}{210}$

24) ABC Corporation earned only $280,000 during the previous year, seven–thirds only of the management's predicted income. How much earning did the management predict?

    A. $440,000

    B. $220,000

    C. $120,000

    D. $110,000

25) How many square feet of tile is needed for 17 feet to 17 feet room?

    A. 98 Square Feet

    B. 890 Square Feet

    C. 189 Square Feet

    D. 289 Square Feet

26) Solve. $\frac{1}{3} + \frac{5}{6} - \frac{2}{12} =$

    A. $\frac{1}{6}$

    B. $\frac{5}{12}$

    C. 1

    D. 12

27) Of the 2,000 videos available for rent at a certain video store, 400 are comedies.

   What percent of the videos are comedies?

   A. $2\frac{1}{20}$ %

   B. 40%

   C. 12%

   D. 20%

28) How many 5 × 5 squares can fit inside a rectangle with a height of 75 and width

   of 20?

   A. 60

   B. 96

   C. 150

   D. 240

29) William keeps track of the length of each fish that he catches. Following are

   the lengths in inches of the fish that he caught one day: 12, 12, 5, 11, 5, 8, 15

   What is the median fish length that William caught that day?

   A. 15 Inches

   B. 8 Inches

   C. 5 Inches

   D. 11 Inches

30) $17 + [5 \times 8] \div 4 =?$

   A. 25

   B. 27

   C. 20

   D. 29

"This is the end of Practice Test 3"

Smarter Balanced Assessment Consortium

SBAC Practice Test 4

Mathematics

GRADE 5

❖ **30 Questions**

❖ **There is no time limit for this practice test.**

❖ **Calculators are NOT permitted for this practice test**

Administered *Month Year*

1) Jack added 8 to the product of 12 and 23. What is this sum?

   A. 94

   B. 148

   C. 284

   D. 1,240

2) Joe makes $6.75 per hour at his work. If he works 4 hours, how much money will he earn?

   A. $32

   B. $30

   C. $26

   D. $27

3) What is the value of $9 - 6\frac{1}{2}$?

   A. $\frac{25}{2}$

   B. $2\frac{1}{2}$

   C. $-\frac{1}{2}$

   D. $\frac{19}{2}$

4) The bride and groom invited 150 guests for their wedding. 120 guests arrived.

What percent of the guest list was not present?

A. 1.20%

B. 80%

C. 120%

D. 20%

5) Frank wants to compare these two measurements.

41.045 kg ☐ 41,054 g

Which symbol should he use?

A. <

B. ≠

C. =

D. >

6) Aria was hired to teach three identical 5th grade math courses, which entailed being present in the classroom 15 hours altogether. At $23 per class hour, how much did Aria earn for teaching one course?

A. $55

B. $115

C. $215

D. $1,115

7) In a classroom of 70 students, 42 are male. What percentage of the class is female?

A. 28%

B. 42%

C. 40%

D. 35%

8) In a party, 11 soft drinks are required for every 16 guests. If there are 144 guests, how many soft drinks are required?

A. 89

B. 49

C. 99

D. 109

9) You are asked to chart the temperature during an 8–hour period to give the average. These are your results:

7 am: 4 degrees	11 am: 27 degrees
8 am: 5 degrees	12 pm: 34 degrees
9 am: 19 degrees	1 pm: 30 degrees
10 am: 29 degrees	2 pm: 28 degrees

What is the average temperature?

A. 22

B. 24

C. 30

D. 36

10) While at work, Emma checks her email once every 40 minutes. In 12 hours, how many times does she check her email?

A. 16 Times

B. 18 Times

C. 9 Times

D. 12 Times

11) In a classroom of 30 students, 18 are male. About what percentage of the class is female?

A. 15%

B. 20%

C. 40%

D. 60%

12) A florist has 799 flowers. How many full bouquets of 17 flowers can he make?

A. 37

B. 35

C. 48

D. 47

13) What is 7,146.59857 rounded to the nearest tenth?

A. 7,146.598

B. 7,146.6

C. 7,146

D. 7,146.59

14) If a rectangular swimming pool has a perimeter of 94 feet and it is 28 feet wide, what is its area?

A. 325 square feet

B. 1,064 square feet

C. 1,235 square feet

D. 532 square feet

15) What is the volume of the following rectangle prism?

A. 92 ft^3

B. 16 ft^3

C. 56 ft^3

D. 112 ft^3

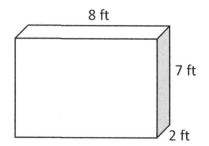

8 ft

7 ft

2 ft

16) A circle has a diameter of 8 inches. What is its approximate circumference? (π = 3.14)

A. 12.52 inches

B. 25.12 inches

C. 25.75 inches

D. 12.75 inches

17) How long is the line segment shown on the number line below?

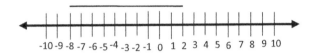

    A. 10

    B. 2

    C. 6

    D. 11

18) If $x = -7$, which equation is true?

    A. $x(2x + 8) = 50$

    B. $2(9 - x) = 32$

    C. $5(4x + 18) = 17$

    D. $2x - 18 = -35$

19) Peter traveled 320 miles in 8 hours and Jason traveled 630 miles in 9 hours.

    What is the ratio of the average speed of Peter to average speed of Jason?

    A. 4: 7

    B. 2: 7

    C. 4: 9

    D. 7: 4

20) A woman owns a dog walking business. If 2 workers can walk 10 dogs, how many dogs can 8 workers walk?

   A. 36

   B. 40

   C. 20

   D. 18

21) Which list shows the fractions listed in order from least to greatest?

$$\frac{1}{3}, \frac{1}{15}, \frac{1}{11}, \frac{1}{7}$$

   A. $\frac{1}{11}, \frac{1}{3}, \frac{1}{15}, \frac{1}{7}$

   B. $\frac{1}{7}, \frac{1}{15}, \frac{1}{3}, \frac{1}{11}$

   C. $\frac{1}{3}, \frac{1}{7}, \frac{1}{11}, \frac{1}{15}$

   D. $\frac{1}{15}, \frac{1}{11}, \frac{1}{7}, \frac{1}{3}$

22) What are the coordinates of the intersection of $x-axis$ and the $y-axis$ on a coordinate plane?

   A. $(0, -8)$

   B. $(8, 0)$

   C. $(0, 0)$

   D. $(0, 8)$

23) In a triangle ABC the measure of angle ACB is 48° and the measure of angle CAB is 87°. What is the measure of angle ABC?

    A. 145

    B. 45

    C. 65

    D. 105

24) David's motorcycle stalled at the beach and he called the towing company. They charged him $ 2.75 per mile for the first 14 miles and then $3.05 per mile for each mile over 14. David was 20 miles from the motorcycle repair shop. How much was David's towing bill?

    A. $46.6

    B. $125.6

    C. $56.8

    D. $65.35

25) A car uses 13 gallons of gas to travel 546 miles. How many miles per gallon does the car get?

    A. 39 miles per gallon

    B. 45 miles per gallon

    C. 42 miles per gallon

    D. 44 miles per gallon

26) Seven out of 49 students had to go to summer school. What is the ratio of students who did not have to go to summer school expressed, in its lowest terms?

A. $\frac{6}{7}$

B. $\frac{1}{7}$

C. $\frac{1}{6}$

D. $\frac{2}{7}$

27) A steak dinner at a restaurant costs $9.25. If a man buys a steak dinner for himself and 5 friends, what will the total cost be?

A. $50.5

B. $55.5

C. $46.25

D. $36.75

28) If 4 garbage trucks can collect the trash of 28 homes in a day. How many trucks are needed to collect in 56 houses?

A. 10

B. 15

C. 7

D. 8

29) A barista averages making 6 cups of coffee per hour. At this rate, how many hours will it take until she's made 390 cups of coffee?

   A. 56

   B. 65

   C. 85

   D. 66

30) Ava needs $\frac{1}{5}$ f an ounce of salt to make 1 cup of dip for fries. How many cups of dip will she be able to make if she has 68 ounces of salt?

   A. 73

   B. 170

   C. 320

   D. 340

"This is the end of Practice Test 4"

Smarter Balanced Assessment Consortium

SBAC Practice Test 5

Mathematics

GRADE 5

❖ **30 Questions**

❖ **There is no time limit for this practice test.**

❖ **Calculators are NOT permitted for this practice test**

Administered *Month Year*

1) The drivers at G & G trucking must report the mileage on their trucks each week. The mileage reading of Ed's vehicle was 64,587 at the beginning of one week, and 65,632 at the end of the same week. What was the total number of miles driven by Ed that week?

   A. 149 MILES

   B. 145 MILES

   C. 1,045 MILES

   D. 1,049 MILES

2) Camille uses a 30% off coupon when buying a sweater that costs $60. How much does she pay?

   A. $42

   B. $45

   C. $42.50

   D. $43

3) The area of a rectangle is D square feet and its length is 10 feet. Which equation represents W, the width of the rectangle in feet?

   A. $W = \dfrac{D}{10}$

   B. $W = \dfrac{10}{D}$

   C. $W = 10D$

   D. $W = 10 + D$

4) A baker uses 2 eggs to bake a cake. How many cakes will he be able to bake with 180 eggs?

   A. 80

   B. 90

   C. 65

   D. 45

5) Which list shows the fractions in order from least to greatest?

$$\frac{3}{7}, \frac{2}{3}, \frac{4}{10}, \frac{1}{8}, \frac{5}{13}$$

   A. $\frac{3}{7}, \frac{2}{3}, \frac{4}{10}, \frac{1}{8}, \frac{5}{13}$

   B. $\frac{5}{13}, \frac{1}{8}, \frac{3}{7}, \frac{2}{3}, \frac{4}{10}$

   C. $\frac{4}{10}, \frac{3}{7}, \frac{2}{3}, \frac{1}{8}, \frac{5}{13}$

   D. $\frac{1}{8}, \frac{5}{13}, \frac{4}{10}, \frac{3}{7}, \frac{2}{3}$

6) Which statement about 4 multiplied by $\frac{5}{3}$ is true?

   A. The product is between 4 and 5

   B. The product is between 6 and 7

   C. The product is more than $\frac{23}{3}$

   D. The product is between $\frac{14}{3}$ and 5

7) A shirt costing $190 is discounted 5%. Which of the following expressions can be used to find the selling price of the shirt?

   A. (190) (0.85)

   B. (190) – 190 (0.10)

   C. (190) (0.05) – (190) (0.05)

   D. (190) (0.95)

8) Which of the following angles is acute?

   A. 90 Degrees

   B. 145 Degrees

   C. 180 Degrees

   D. 30 Degrees

9) If A = 10, then which of the following equations are correct?

   A. A + 40 = 400

   B. A ÷ 40 = 400

   C. 40 × A = 400

   D. A – 40 = 400

10) The perimeter of the trapezoid below is 100. What is its area?

   A. 264

   B. 528

   C. 176

   D. 76

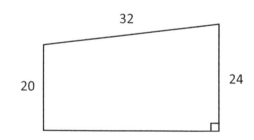

11) In a bag, there are 90 cards. Of these cards, 10 cards are white. What fraction of the cards are white?

A. $\frac{1}{9}$

B. $\frac{4}{30}$

C. $\frac{32}{64}$

D. $\frac{1}{10}$

12) A rope weighs 700 grams per meter of length. What is the weight in kilograms of 5.5 meters of this rope? (1 kilograms = 1000 grams)

A. 0.0385

B. 0.385

C. 3.85

D. 3,850

13) 13) Lily and Ella are in a pancake–eating contest. Lily can eat two pancakes per minute, while Ella can eat $2\frac{1}{4}$ pancakes per minute. How many total pancakes can they eat in 8 minutes?

A. 16 Pancakes

B. 18. Pancakes

C. 34.5 Pancakes

D. 34 Pancakes

14) How many $\frac{1}{8}$ cup servings are in a package of cheese that contains $3\frac{3}{4}$ cups altogether?

   A. $\frac{15}{8}$

   B. 30

   C. 15

   D. $\frac{8}{15}$

15) With what number must 7.326367 be multiplied in order to obtain the number 732,636.7?

   A. 100

   B. 1,000

   C. 10,000

   D. 100,000

16) What is the volume of this box?

   A. 70 cm^3

   B. 90 cm^3

   C. 280 cm^3

   D. 200 cm^3

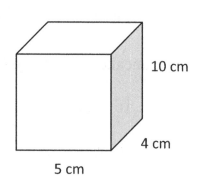

10 cm

4 cm

5 cm

17) 50 is What percent of 80?

   A. 20 %

   B. 62 %

   C. 62.5 %

   D. 150 %

18) The area of a circle is 144π. What is the circumference of the circle?

   A. 48 π

   B. 24 π

   C. 121 π

   D. 64 π

19) The distance between cities A and B is approximately 1,900 miles. If Alice drive an average of 76 miles per hour, how many hours will it take Alice to drive from city A to city B?

   A. Approximately 31 Hours

   B. Approximately 25 Hours

   C. Approximately 29 Hours

   D. Approximately 27 Hours

20) 5 yards 4 feet and 12 inches equals to how many inches?

   A. 96

   B. 420

   C. 240

   D. 370

21) Which expression has a value of -12?

    A. $10 - (-5) + (-27)$

    B. $4 + (-5) \times (-4)$

    C. $-2 \times (-2) + (-5) \times (-11)$

    D. $(-3) \times (-8) + 5$

22) Solve. $\frac{7}{9} \times \frac{3}{7} =$

    A. $\frac{1}{3}$

    B. $\frac{10}{40}$

    C. $\frac{30}{70}$

    D. $\frac{1}{4}$

23) The length of a rectangle is $\frac{4}{9}$ of inches and the width of the rectangle is $\frac{3}{16}$ of inches. What is the area of that rectangle?

    A. $\frac{1}{2}$

    B. $\frac{1}{12}$

    C. $\frac{10}{36}$

    D. $\frac{12}{124}$

24) ABC Corporation earned only $250,000 during the previous year, five–second only of the management's predicted income. How much earning did the management predict?

    A. $140,000

    B. $200,000

    C. $100,000

    D. $240,000

25) How many square feet of tile is needed for 20 feet to 20 feet room?

    A. 40 Square Feet

    B. 100 Square Feet

    C. 200 Square Feet

    D. 400 Square Feet

26) Solve. $\frac{1}{2} + \frac{8}{15} - \frac{1}{30} =$

    A. $\frac{9}{30}$

    B. $\frac{2}{10}$

    C. 1

    D. 30

27) Of the 4,000 videos available for rent at a certain video store, 800 are comedies. What percent of the videos are comedies?

    A. $18\frac{1}{2}\%$

    B. 25%

    C. 22%

    D. 20%

28) How many 4×4 squares can fit inside a rectangle with a height of 64 and width of 30?

    A. 120

    B. 192

    C. 160

    D. 920

29) William keeps track of the length of each fish that he catches. Following are the lengths in inches of the fish that he caught one day: 10, 11, 4, 9, 4, 6, 13

What is the median fish length that William caught that day?

    A. 13 Inches

    B. 4 Inches

    C. 6 Inches

    D. 9 Inches

30) $18 + [4 \times 3] \div 3 =?$

    A. 21

    B. 22

    C. 30

    D. 19

"This is the end of Practice Test 5"

Smarter Balanced Assessment Consortium

SBAC Practice Test 6

Mathematics

GRADE 5

❖ **30 Questions**

❖ **There is no time limit for this practice test.**

❖ **Calculators are NOT permitted for this practice test**

Administered *Month Year*

1) Jack added 6 to the product of 10 and 24. What is this sum?

    A. 84

    B. 154

    C. 246

    D. 1,440

2) Joe makes $5.5 per hour at his work. If he works 8 hours, how much money will he earn?

    A. $33

    B. $32

    C. $36

    D. $44

3) What is the value of $10 - 5\frac{1}{3}$?

    A. $\frac{46}{3}$

    B. $4\frac{2}{3}$

    C. $-\frac{1}{3}$

    D. $\frac{24}{3}$

4) The bride and groom invited 240 guests for their wedding. 210 guests arrived.

What percent of the guest list was not present?

A. 1.25%

B. 30%

C. 87.5%

D. 12.5%

5) Frank wants to compare these two measurements.

23.023 kg ☐ 23,032 g

Which symbol should he use?

A. <

B. >

C. ≠

D. =

6) Aria was hired to teach six identical 5th grade math courses, which entailed being present in the classroom 36 hours altogether. At $25 per class hour, how much did Aria earn for teaching one course?

A. $50

B. $150

C. $300

D. $1,500

7) In a classroom of 60 students, 40 are male. What percentage of the class is female?

    A. 15.7%

    B. 35.7%

    C. 33.3%

    D. 42.7%

8) In a party, 10 soft drinks are required for every 18 guests. If there are 153 guests, how many soft drinks are required?

    A. 15

    B. 35

    C. 85

    D. 125

9) You are asked to chart the temperature during an 8–hour period to give the average. These are your results:

7 am: 2 degrees	11 am: 28 degrees
8 am: 4 degrees	12 pm: 33 degrees
9 am: 21 degrees	1 pm: 31 degrees
10 am: 27 degrees	2 pm: 30 degrees

What is the average temperature?

    A. 22

    B. 26

    C. 32

    D. 34

10) While at work, Emma checks her email once every 60 minutes. In 6 hours, how many times does she check her email?

A. 10 Times

B. 6 Times

C. 8 Times

D. 5 Times

11) In a classroom of 70 students, 49 are male. About what percentage of the class is female?

A. 30%

B. 40%

C. 30%

D. 45%

12) A florist has 735 flowers. How many full bouquets of 15 flowers can he make?

A. 43

B. 45

C. 47

D. 49

13) What is 9,258.48991 rounded to the nearest tenth?

A. 9,258.489

B. 9,258.5

C. 9,258

D. 9,258.48

14) If a rectangular swimming pool has a perimeter of 134 feet and it is 37 feet wide, what is its area?

A. 1,030 square feet

B. 2,220 square feet

C. 1,015 square feet

D. 1,110 square feet

15) What is the volume of the following rectangle prism?

A. 33 ft³

B. 99 ft³

C. 27 ft³

D. 297 ft³

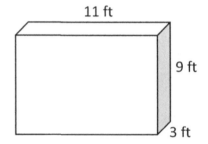

16) A circle has a diameter of 12 inches. What is its approximate circumference?

($\pi = 3.14$)

A. 18.84 inches

B. 37.68 inches

C. 27.68 inches

D. 75.36 inches

17) How long is the line segment shown on the number line below?

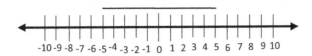

    A. 10

    B. 5

    C. 8

    D. 12

18) If $x = -4$, which equation is true?

    A. $x(4x - 5) = 75$

    B. $4(6 - x) = 40$

    C. $3(2x + 5) = 12$

    D. $4x - 6 = -20$

19) Peter traveled 200 miles in 5 hours and Jason traveled 210 miles in 7 hours.

What is the ratio of the average speed of Peter to average speed of Jason?

    A. 4: 3

    B. 3: 5

    C. 9: 7

    D. 5: 3

20) A woman owns a dog walking business. If 4 workers can walk 8 dogs, how many dogs can 9 workers walk?

   A. 16

   B. 18

   C. 9

   D. 14

21) Which list shows the fractions listed in order from least to greatest?

$$\frac{1}{2}, \frac{1}{9}, \frac{1}{8}, \frac{1}{5}$$

   A. $\frac{1}{8}, \frac{1}{2}, \frac{1}{9}, \frac{1}{5}$

   B. $\frac{1}{5}, \frac{1}{9}, \frac{1}{2}, \frac{1}{8}$

   C. $\frac{1}{2}, \frac{1}{5}, \frac{1}{8}, \frac{1}{9}$

   D. $\frac{1}{9}, \frac{1}{8}, \frac{1}{5}, \frac{1}{2}$

22) What are the coordinates of the intersection of $x-axis$ and the $y-axis$ on a coordinate plane?

   A. $(0, -1)$

   B. $(1, 0)$

   C. $(0, 0)$

   D. $(0, 1)$

23) In a triangle ABC the measure of angle ACB is 45° and the measure of angle CAB is 90°. What is the measure of angle ABC?

A. 135

B. 45

C. 55

D. 65

24) David's motorcycle stalled at the beach and he called the towing company. They charged him $ 3.25 per mile for the first 25 miles and then $4.06 per mile for each mile over 25. David was 30 miles from the motorcycle repair shop. How much was David's towing bill?

A. $95.55

B. $110.55

C. $101.55

D. $125.55

25) A car uses 19 gallons of gas to travel 608 miles. How many miles per gallon does the car get?

A. 29 miles per gallon

B. 22 miles per gallon

C. 32 miles per gallon

D. 34 miles per gallon

26) Six out of 24 students had to go to summer school. What is the ratio of students who did not have to go to summer school expressed, in its lowest terms?

    A. $\frac{3}{4}$

    B. $\frac{1}{4}$

    C. $\frac{1}{2}$

    D. $\frac{1}{3}$

27) A steak dinner at a restaurant costs $7.75. If a man buys a steak dinner for himself and 2 friends, what will the total cost be?

    A. $32.50

    B. $23.25

    C. $25.25

    D. $15.50

28) If 6 garbage trucks can collect the trash of 48 homes in a day. How many trucks are needed to collect in 72 houses?

    A. 11

    B. 10

    C. 4

    D. 9

29) A barista averages making 9 cups of coffee per hour. At this rate, how many hours will it take until she's made 783 cups of coffee?

   A. 78

   B. 87

   C. 86

   D. 76

30) Ava needs $\frac{1}{6}$ f an ounce of salt to make 1 cup of dip for fries. How many cups of dip will she be able to make if she has 80 ounces of salt?

   A. 86

   B. 150

   C. 360

   D. 480

"This is the end of Practice Test 6"

Answer Keys

SBAC Practice Tests

✳ Now, it's time to review your results to see where you went wrong and what areas you need to improve!

Practice Test - 1					
1	C	11	A	21	A
2	A	12	C	22	A
3	A	13	D	23	B
4	B	14	B	24	C
5	D	15	C	25	D
6	B	16	D	26	C
7	D	17	C	27	D
8	D	18	B	28	A
9	A	19	B	29	D
10	B	20	C	30	B

Practice Test - 2					
1	C	11	C	21	D
2	D	12	D	22	C
3	B	13	B	23	B
4	D	14	D	24	C
5	D	15	D	25	C
6	B	16	B	26	A
7	C	17	A	27	B
8	C	18	B	28	D
9	A	19	A	29	B
10	B	20	B	30	D

Practice Test - 3

1	C	11	A	21	A
2	A	12	C	22	A
3	A	13	D	23	B
4	B	14	B	24	C
5	D	15	D	25	D
6	B	16	D	26	C
7	D	17	C	27	D
8	D	18	B	28	A
9	C	19	B	29	D
10	B	20	C	30	B

Practice Test - 4

1	C	11	C	21	D
2	D	12	D	22	C
3	B	13	B	23	B
4	D	14	D	24	C
5	A	15	D	25	C
6	B	16	B	26	A
7	C	17	A	27	B
8	C	18	B	28	D
9	A	19	A	29	B
10	B	20	B	30	D

Practice Test - 5

1	C	11	A	21	A
2	A	12	C	22	A
3	A	13	D	23	B
4	B	14	B	24	C
5	D	15	D	25	D
6	B	16	D	26	C
7	D	17	C	27	D
8	D	18	B	28	A
9	C	19	B	29	D
10	B	20	C	30	B

Practice Test - 6

1	C	11	C	21	D
2	D	12	D	22	C
3	B	13	B	23	B
4	D	14	D	24	C
5	A	15	D	25	C
6	B	16	B	26	A
7	C	17	A	27	B
8	C	18	B	28	D
9	A	19	A	29	B
10	B	20	B	30	D

Answers and

Explanations

Practice Test 1

SBAC - Mathematics

Answers and Explanations

1) Answer: C.

To find the answer, subtract 43,907 from 44,053.

$44,053 - 43,907 = 146\ miles$

2) Answer: A.

Let x be the new price after discount.

$x = 30 \times (100 - 40)\% = 50 \times 60\% = 30 \times 0.60 = 18 \Rightarrow x = \$18$

3) Answer: A.

Use area of rectangle formula.

Area of a rectangle $= width \times length \Rightarrow D = w \times l \Rightarrow w = \dfrac{D}{l} = \dfrac{D}{7}$

4) Answer: B.

3 eggs for 1 cake. Therefore, 210 eggs can be used for $(210 \div 3)$ 70 cakes.

5) Answer: D.

To list the fractions from least to greatest, you can convert the fractions to decimal.

$\dfrac{3}{4} = 0.75; \dfrac{6}{7} = 0.86; \dfrac{2}{10} = 0.2; \dfrac{1}{2} = 0.5; \dfrac{6}{14} = 0.43$

$\dfrac{2}{10} = 0.2, \dfrac{6}{14} = 0.43, \dfrac{1}{2} = 0.5, \dfrac{3}{4} = 0.75, \dfrac{6}{7} = 0.86$

Option D shows the fractions in order from least to greatest.

6) Answer: B.

5 multiplied by $\dfrac{4}{3} = \dfrac{20}{3} = 6.66$, therefore, only choice B is correct.

7) Answer: D.

To find the selling price, multiply the price by (100% – rate of discount).

Then: (150) (100% – 10%) = (150) (0.9) = 135

8) Answer: D.

An obtuse angle is any angle larger than 90 degrees. From the options provided, only D (120 degrees) is larger than 90.

9) Answer: A.

Plug in 30 for A in the equations. Only option A works.

$A + 30 = 60$

$30 + 30 = 60$

10) Answer: B.

First, find the missing side of the trapezoid. The perimeter of the trapezoid below is 50.

Therefore, the missing side of the trapezoid (its height) is:

$50 - 10 - 16 - 12 = 50 - 38 = 12$

Area of a trapezoid: A = $\frac{1}{2}$ h (b1 + b2)

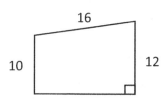

$= \frac{1}{2} (12) (10 + 12) = 132$

11) Answer: A.

There are 40 cards in the bag and 8 of them are white. Then, 8 out of 40 cards are white.

You can write this as: $\frac{8}{40}$. To simplify this fraction, divide both numerator and

denominator by 13. Then: $\frac{8}{40} = \frac{1}{5}$

12) Answer: C.

1 meter of the rope = 500 grams

12.2 meter of the rope = 12.2 $\times$ 500 = 6,100 grams = 6.1 kilograms

13) Answer: D.

Lily eats 3 pancakes in 1 minute ⇒ Lily eats 3 × 5 pancakes in 5 minutes (15).

Ella eats 2 ½ pancakes in 1 minute ⇒ Ella eats 2 ½ × 5 pancakes in 5 minutes

($\frac{25}{2}$ =12.5).

In total Lily and Ella eat 15 + 12.5=27.5 pancakes in 5 minutes.

14) Answer: B.

To solve this problem, divide $5\frac{1}{2}$ by $\frac{1}{4}$.

$5\frac{1}{2} \div \frac{1}{4} = \frac{11}{2} \div \frac{1}{4} = \frac{11}{2} \times \frac{4}{1} = 22$

15) Answer: C.

The question is that number 52,536.91 is how many times of number 5.253691. The answer is 10,000.

16) Answer: D.

Use volume of cube formula.

Volume= $length \times width \times height \Rightarrow V = 7 \times 5 \times 9 \Rightarrow V = 315 \; cm^3$

17) Answer: C.

Use percent formula: $\text{part} = \frac{\text{percent}}{100} \times \text{whole}$

$25 = \frac{\text{percent}}{100} \times 40 \Rightarrow 25 = \frac{\text{percent} \times 40}{100} \Rightarrow 25 = \frac{\text{percent} \times 4}{10}$, multiply both sides by 10.

$250 = \text{percent} \times 4$, divide both sides by 4 $\Rightarrow 62.5 = \text{percent}$

18) Answer: B.

Use area and circumference of circle formula.

Area of a circle $= \pi r^2 \Rightarrow 36\pi = \pi r^2 \Rightarrow r = 6$

Circumference of a circle $= 2\pi r \Rightarrow C = 2 \times 6 \times \pi \Rightarrow C = 12\pi$

19) Answer: B.

Alice drives 56 miles in one hour. Therefore, she drives 1960 miles in about $(1960 \div 56)$ 35 hours.

20) Answer: C.

10 yards = $10 \times 36 = 360$ inches

3 feet = $3 \times 12 = 36$ inches

10 yards 3 feet and 4 inches = 360 inches + 36 inches + 4 inches = 400 inches

21) Answer: A.

Simplify each option provided using order of operations rules.

A. $7 - (-3) + (-17) = 7 + 3 - 17 = -7$

B. $1 + (-3) \times (-2) = 1 + 6 = 7$

C. $-6 \times (-6) + (-2) \times (-12) = 36 + 24 = 60$

D. $(-2) \times (-7) + 4 = 14 + 4 = 18$

Only option A is -7.

22) Answer: A.

$$\frac{6}{8} \times \frac{4}{6} = \frac{6 \times 4}{8 \times 6} = \frac{24}{48} = \frac{1}{2}$$

23) Answer: B.

Use area of rectangle formula.

$$Area = length \times width \Rightarrow A = \frac{5}{6} \times \frac{2}{15} \Rightarrow A = \frac{1}{9} \text{ inches}$$

24) Answer: C.

ABC Corporation's income $= \frac{3}{2}$ management's predicted income.

$300,000 $= \frac{3}{2}$ management's predicted income

management's predicted income $= \$300,000 \times \frac{2}{3} = \$200,000$

25) Answer: D.

Find the area of the room which is a square. Use area of square formula.

$$S = a^2 \Rightarrow S = 16 \text{ feet} \times 16 \text{ feet} = 256 \text{ square feet}$$

26) Answer: C.

$$\frac{1}{2} + \frac{4}{7} - \frac{1}{14} = \frac{(7 \times 1) + (2 \times 4) - (1 \times 1)}{14} = \frac{14}{14} = 1$$

27) Answer: D.

Use percent formula: $\text{part} = \frac{\text{percent}}{100} \times \text{whole}$

$900 = \frac{\text{percent}}{100} \times 3600 \Rightarrow 900 = \text{percent} \times 36 \Rightarrow \text{percent} = 25$

28) Answer: A.

Use area of rectangle formula. $A = a \times b \Rightarrow A = 52 \times 18 \Rightarrow A = 936$

Divide the area by 9 ($3 \times 3 = 9$ squares) to find the number of squares needed.

$936 \div 9 = 104$

29) Answer: D.

Write the numbers in order: 9, 9, 10, 14, 15, 16, 18

Median is the number in the middle. Therefore, the median is 14.

30) Answer: B.

Use PEMDAS (order of operation): $6 + [6 \times 5] \div 2 = 6 + (30) \div 2 = 6 + (30 \div 2) = 21$

Practice Test 2

SBAC - Mathematics

Answers and Explanations

1) Answer: C.

$16 + (14 \times 22) = 16 + 308 = 324$

2) Answer: D.

1 hour: $4.75

6 hours: $6 \times \$4.75 = \$28.5$

3) Answer: B.

$5 - 3\frac{2}{9} = \frac{45}{9} - \frac{29}{9} = \frac{16}{9}$

4) Answer: D.

The number of guests that are not present are: $(230 - 190)$ 40 out of $230 = \frac{40}{230}$

Change the fraction to percent: $\frac{40}{230} \times 100\% = 17.4\%$

5) Answer: D.

Each kilogram is 1,000 grams.

19,023 grams $= \frac{19,023}{1,000} = 19.023$ kilograms. Therefore, two amounts provided are equal.

6) Answer: B.

Aria teaches 24 hours for three identical courses. Therefore, she teaches 8 hours for each course. Aria earns $20 per hour. Therefore, she earned $160 (8×20) for each course.

7) Answer: C.

The number of female students in the class is: $(50 - 25)$ 25 out of $50 = \frac{25}{50}$

Change the fraction to percent: $\frac{25}{50} \times 100\% = 50\%$

8) Answer: C.

Write a proportion and solve.

$\frac{8 \text{ soft drinks}}{12 \text{ guests}} = \frac{x}{156 \text{ guests}} \Rightarrow x = \frac{156 \times 8}{12} \Rightarrow x = 104$

9) Answer: A.

average (mean) = $\frac{\text{sum of terms}}{\text{number of terms}}$ ⇒ average = $\frac{3+6+23+29+31+34+34+32}{8}$ ⇒ average = 24

10) Answer: B.

Every 90 minutes Emma checks her email.

In 5 hours (450 minutes), Emma checks her email (450 ÷ 90) 5 times.

11) Answer: C.

There are 66 students in the class. 30 of the are male and 36 of them are female. 36 out of 66 are female. Then:

$\frac{36}{66} = \frac{x}{100}$ → 3,600 = 66x → x = 3,600 ÷ 66 = 54.54 … ≈ 55%

12) Answer: D.

Divide the number flowers by 13: 585 ÷ 13 = 45

13) Answer: B.

Rounding decimals is similar to rounding other numbers. If the hundredths and thousandths places of a decimal is forty-nine or less, they are dropped, and the tenths place does not change. For example, rounding 0.843 to the nearest tenth would give 0.8. Therefore, 6,123.48245 rounded to the nearest tenth is 6,123.5.

14) Answer: D.

Perimeter of rectangle formula:

$P = 2\,(length + width) \Rightarrow 124 = 2\,(l + 24) \Rightarrow l = 38$

Area of rectangle formula: $A = length \times width \Rightarrow A = 38 \times 24 \Rightarrow A = 912$

15) Answer: D.

Use volume of rectangle prism formula.

$V = length \times width \times height \Rightarrow V = 7 \times 5 \times 6 \Rightarrow V = 210$

16) Answer: B.

The diameter of the circle is 4 inches. Therefore, the radius of the circle is 2 inches. Use circumference of circle formula. $C = 2\pi r \Rightarrow C = 2 \times 3.14 \times 2 \Rightarrow C = 12.56$

17) Answer: A.

The line segment is from 3 to −7. Therefore, the line is 9 units.

$3 - (-7) = 3 + 7 = 10$

18) Answer: B.

Plug in $x = -2$ in each equation.

A. $x(2x - 4) = 50 \rightarrow (-2)(2(-2) - 4) = (-2) \times (-4 - 4) = 16$

B. $8(4 - x) = 48 \rightarrow 8(4 - (-2) = 8(6) = 48$

C. $2(4x + 6) = 10 \rightarrow 2(4(-2) + 6) = 2(-8 + 6) = 8$

D. $6x - 2 = -23 \rightarrow 6(-2) - 2 = -12 - 2 = -14$

Only option B.

19) Answer: A.

Peter's speed $= \dfrac{160}{4} = 40$

Jason's speed $= \dfrac{240}{8} = 30$

$\dfrac{\textit{The average speed of peter}}{\textit{The average speed of Jason}} = \dfrac{40}{30}$ equals to: $\dfrac{4}{3}$ or $4:3$

20) Answer: B.

3 workers can walk 9 dogs $\Rightarrow$ 1 workers can walk 3 dogs.

6 workers can walk (6×3) 18 dogs.

21) Answer: D.

In fractions, when denominators increase, the value of fractions decrease and as much as numerators increase, the value of fractions increase. Therefore, the least one of this list is: $\dfrac{1}{10}$ and the greatest one of this list is: $\dfrac{1}{3}$

22) Answer: C.

The horizontal axis in the coordinate plane is called the $x - axis$. The vertical axis is called the $y - axis$. The point at which the two axes intersect is called the origin. The origin is at 0 on the $x - axis$ and 0 on the $y - axis$.

23) Answer: B.

All angles in every triangle add up to $180°$. Let x be the angle ABC. Then: $180 = 65 + 35 + x \Rightarrow x = 80°$

24) Answer: C.

$3.75 per mile for the first 20 miles. Therefore, the cost for the first 20 miles is:

20 × $3.75 = $75

$4.15 per mile for each mile over 20, therefore, 8 miles over 20 miles cost:

8 × $4.15 = $33.20

In total, David pays: $75 + $33.20 = $108.20

25) Answer: C.

Write a proportion and solve.

15 gallons: 675 miles ⇒ 1 gallon: 675 ÷ 15 = 45 miles

26) Answer: A.

The students that had to go to summer school is 5 out of 30 $= \frac{5}{35} = \frac{1}{7}$

Therefore $\frac{6}{7}$ students did not have to go to summer school.

27) Answer: B.

4 steak dinners = 4 × $8.5 = $34

28) Answer: D.

4 garbage trucks can collect the trash of 32 homes. Then, one garbage truck can collect the trash of 8 homes.

To collect trash of 80 houses, 10 (80 ÷ 8) garbage trucks are required.

29) Answer: B.

12 cups: 1 hour

1080 cups: 1080 ÷ 12 = 90 hours

30) Answer: D.

Write a proportion and solve.

$\frac{\frac{1}{5}}{60} = \frac{1}{x} \Rightarrow x = 60 \times 5 = 300$

Practice Test 3

SBAC - Mathematics

Answers and Explanations

1) Answer: C.

To find the answer, subtract 44,476 from 45,521.

$45,521 - 44,476 = 1,045 \; miles$

2) Answer: A.

Let x be the new price after discount.

$x = 80 \times (100 - 20)\% = 80 \times 80\% = 80 \times 0.80 = 64 \Rightarrow x = \$64$

3) Answer: A.

Use area of rectangle formula.

Area of a rectangle $= width \times length \Rightarrow D = w \times l \Rightarrow w = \dfrac{D}{l} = \dfrac{D}{17}$

4) Answer: B.

3 eggs for 1 cake. Therefore, 330 eggs can be used for $(330 \div 3)$ 110 cakes.

5) Answer: D.

To list the fractions from least to greatest, you can convert the fractions to decimal.

$\dfrac{4}{5} = 0.8; \; \dfrac{9}{10} = 0.9; \; \dfrac{1}{6} = 0.167; \; \dfrac{2}{5} = 0.4; \; \dfrac{3}{8} = 0.375$

$\dfrac{1}{6} = 0.167, \; \dfrac{3}{8} = 0.375, \; \dfrac{2}{5} = 0.4, \; \dfrac{4}{5} = 0.8, \; \dfrac{9}{10} = 0.9$

Option D shows the fractions in order from least to greatest.

6) Answer: B.

3 multiplied by $\dfrac{5}{4} = \dfrac{15}{4} = 3.75$, therefore, only choice B is correct.

7) Answer: D.

To find the selling price, multiply the price by (100% – rate of discount).

Then: $(150) (100\% - 6\%) = (150) (0.94) = 141$

8) Answer: D.

An acute angle is any angle smaller than 90 degrees.

From the options provided, only D (50 degrees) is smaller than 90.

9) Answer: C.

Plug in 50 for A in the equations. Only option A works.

$A \times 50 = 600$

$12 \times 50 = 600$

10) Answer: B.

First, find the missing side of the trapezoid. The perimeter of the trapezoid below is 40.

Therefore, the missing side of the trapezoid (its height) is:

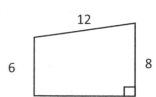

$40 - 12 - 8 - 6 = 40 - 26 = 14$

Area of a trapezoid: $A = \frac{1}{2} h (b1 + b2)$

$= \frac{1}{2} (14) (6 + 8) = 98$

11) Answer: A.

There are 98 cards in the bag and 14 of them are white. Then, 14 out of 98 cards are white. You can write this as: $\frac{14}{98}$. To simplify this fraction, divide both numerator and denominator by 14. Then: $\frac{14}{98} = \frac{1}{7}$

12) Answer: C.

1 meter of the rope = 900 grams

4.5 meter of the rope = $4.5 \times 900 = 4,050$ grams = 4.05 kilograms

13) Answer: D.

Lily eats 3 pancakes in 1 minute $\Rightarrow$ Lily eats 3×9 pancakes in 9 minutes (27).

Ella eats $4\frac{1}{3}$ pancakes in 1 minute $\Rightarrow$ Ella eats $4\frac{1}{3} \times 9$ pancakes in 9 minutes ($\frac{117}{3} = 39$).

In total Lily and Ella eat $27 + 39 = 66$ pancakes in 9 minutes.

14) Answer: B.

To solve this problem, divide $2\frac{1}{3}$ by $\frac{1}{9}$.

$2\frac{1}{3} \div \frac{1}{9} = \frac{7}{3} \div \frac{1}{9} = \frac{7}{3} \times \frac{9}{1} = 21$

15) Answer: D.

The question is that number 986,458.9 is how many times of number 9.864589. The answer is 100,000.

16) Answer: D.

Use volume of cube formula.

Volume= $length \times width \times height \Rightarrow V = 7 \times 5 \times 11 \Rightarrow V = 385 \ cm^3$

17) Answer: C.

Use percent formula: $part = \frac{percent}{100} \times whole$

$15 = \frac{percent}{100} \times 50 \Rightarrow 15 = \frac{percent \times 50}{100} \Rightarrow 15 = \frac{percent \times 5}{10}$, multiply both sides by 10.

$150 = percent \times 5$, divide both sides by 5. $\Rightarrow 30$ percent

18) Answer: B.

Use area and circumference of circle formula.

Area of a circle $= \pi r^2 \Rightarrow 121\pi = \pi r^2 \Rightarrow r = 11$

Circumference of a circle $= 2\pi r \Rightarrow C = 2 \times 11 \times \pi \Rightarrow C = 22\pi$

19) Answer: B.

Alice drives 56 miles in one hour. Therefore, she drives 1,960 miles in about ($1,960 \div 56$) 35 hours.

20) Answer: C.

7 yards = 7 × 36 = 252 inches, 6 feet = 6 × 12 = 72 inches

7 yards 6 feet and 18 inches = 252 inches + 72 inches + 18 inches = 342 inches

21) Answer: A.

Simplify each option provided using order of operations rules.

    A. $7 - (-5) + (-25) = 7 + 5 - 25 = -13$

    B. $3 + (-3) \times (-9) = 3 + 27 = 30$

    C. $-4 \times (-5) + (-2) \times (-10) = 20 + 20 = 40$

    D. $(-7) \times (-4) + 2 = 28 + 2 = 30$

Only option A is -13.

22) Answer: A.

$$\frac{5}{8} \times \frac{2}{5} = \frac{5 \times 2}{8 \times 5} = \frac{10}{40} = \frac{1}{4}$$

23) Answer: B.

Use area of rectangle formula.

Area= $length \times width \Rightarrow A = \frac{7}{10} \times \frac{5}{21} \Rightarrow A = \frac{1}{6}$ inches

24) Answer: C.

ABC Corporation's income $= \frac{7}{3}$ management's predicted income.

$\$280,000 = \frac{7}{3}$ management's predicted income

management's predicted income $= \$280,000 \times \frac{3}{7} = \$120,000$

25) Answer: D.

Find the area of the room which is a square. Use area of square formula.

$S = a^2 \Rightarrow S = 17\ feet \times 17\ feet = 289$ square feet

26) Answer: C.

$$\frac{1}{3} + \frac{5}{6} - \frac{2}{12} = \frac{(1 \times 4)+(2 \times 5)-(2 \times 1)}{12} = \frac{12}{12} = 1$$

27) Answer: D.

Use percent formula: $\text{part} = \frac{\text{percent}}{100} \times \text{whole}$

$400 = \frac{\text{percent}}{100} \times 2,000 \Rightarrow 400 = \text{percent} \times 20 \Rightarrow \text{percent} = 20$

28) Answer: A.

Use area of rectangle formula. $A = a \times b \Rightarrow A = 75 \times 20 \Rightarrow A = 1,500$

Divide the area by 25 ($5 \times 5 = 25$ squares) to find the number of squares needed.

$1,500 \div 25 = 60$

29) Answer: D.

Write the numbers in order: 5, 5, 8, 11, 12, 12, 15

Median is the number in the middle. Therefore, the median is 11.

30) Answer: B.

Use PEMDAS (order of operation): $17 + [5 \times 8] \div 4 = 17 + (40) \div 4 = 17 + (40 \div 4) = 17 + 10 = 27$

Practice Test 4

SBAC - Mathematics

Answers and Explanations

1) Answer: C.

$8 + (12 \times 23) = 8 + 276 = 284$

2) Answer: D.

1 hour: $6.75

4 hours: $4 \times \$6.75 = \$27$

3) Answer: B.

$9 - 6\frac{1}{2} = \frac{18}{2} - \frac{13}{2} = \frac{5}{2} = 2\frac{1}{2}$

4) Answer: D.

The number of guests that are not present are: $(150 - 120)$ 30 out of $150 = \frac{30}{150}$

Change the fraction to percent: $\frac{30}{150} \times 100\% = 20\%$

5) Answer: A.

Each kilogram is 1,000 grams. 41,054 grams $= \frac{41,054}{1,000} = 41.054$ kilograms. Therefore, 41,054 grams are greater than the 23.045 kg.

6) Answer: B.

Aria teaches 15 hours for three identical courses. Therefore, she teaches 5 hours for each course. Aria earns $23 per hour. Therefore, she earned $115 ($5 \times 23$) for each course.

7) Answer: C.

The number of female students in the class is: $(70 - 42)$ 28 out of $70 = \frac{28}{70}$

Change the fraction to percent: $\frac{28}{70} \times 100\% = 40\%$

8) Answer: C.

Write a proportion and solve.

$\frac{11 \text{ soft drinks}}{16 \text{ guests}} = \frac{x}{144 \text{ guests}} \Rightarrow x = \frac{144 \times 11}{16} \Rightarrow x = 99$

9) Answer: A.

$$\text{average (mean)} = \frac{\text{sum of terms}}{\text{number of terms}} \Rightarrow \text{average} = \frac{4+5+19+29+27+34+30+28}{8} \Rightarrow \text{average} = 22$$

10) Answer: B.

Every 40 minutes Emma checks her email.

In 12 hours (720 minutes), Emma checks her email $(720 \div 40)$ 18 times.

11) Answer: C.

There are 30 students in the class. 18 of the are male and 12 of them are female. 12 out of 30 are female. Then:

$$\frac{12}{30} = \frac{x}{100} \rightarrow 1,200 = 30x \rightarrow x = 12,00 \div 30 = 40\%$$

12) Answer: D.

Divide the number flowers by 17: $799 \div 17 = 47$

13) Answer: B.

Rounding decimals is similar to rounding other numbers. If the hundredths and thousandths places of a decimal is fifty-nine or less, they are dropped, and the tenths place does not change. For example, rounding 0.843 to the nearest tenth would give 0.8. Therefore, 7,146.59857 rounded to the nearest tenth is 7,146.6.

14) Answer: D.

Perimeter of rectangle formula:

$$P = 2\,(length + width) \Rightarrow 94 = 2\,(l + 28) \Rightarrow l = 19$$

Area of rectangle formula: $A = length \times width \Rightarrow A = 28 \times 19 \Rightarrow A = 532$

15) Answer: D.

Use volume of rectangle prism formula.

$$V = length \times width \times height \Rightarrow V = 8 \times 2 \times 7 \Rightarrow V = 112$$

16) Answer: B.

The diameter of the circle is 8 inches. Therefore, the radius of the circle is 4 inches. Use circumference of circle formula. $C = 2\pi r \Rightarrow C = 2 \times 3.14 \times 4 \Rightarrow C = 25.12$

17) Answer: A.

The line segment is from 2 to -8. Therefore, the line is 10 units.

$$2 - (-8) = 2 + 8 = 10$$

18) Answer: B.

Plug in $x - 7$ in each equation.

A. $x(2x + 8) = 50 \rightarrow (-7)(2(-7) + 8) = (-7) \times (-14 + 8) = 42$

B. $2(9 - x) = 32 \rightarrow 2(9 - (-7)) = 2(16) = 32$

C. $5(4x + 18) = 17 \rightarrow 5(4(-7) + 18) = 5(-28 + 18) = -50$

D. $2x - 18 = -35 \rightarrow 2(-7) - 18 = -14 - 18 = -32$

Only option B.

19) Answer: A.

Peter's speed $= \dfrac{320}{8} = 40$

Jason's speed $= \dfrac{630}{9} = 70$

$\dfrac{\textit{The average speed of peter}}{\textit{The average speed of Jason}} = \dfrac{40}{70}$ equals to: $\dfrac{4}{7}$ or $4:7$

20) Answer: B.

2 workers can walk 10 dogs $\Rightarrow$ 1 workers can walk 5 dogs.

8 workers can walk (8×5) 40 dogs.

21) Answer: D.

In fractions, when denominators increase, the value of fractions decrease and as much as numerators increase, the value of fractions increase. Therefore, the least one of this list is: $\dfrac{1}{15}$ and the greatest one of this list is: $\dfrac{1}{3}$

22) Answer: C.

The horizontal axis in the coordinate plane is called the $x - axis$. The vertical axis is called the $y - axis$. The point at which the two axes intersect is called the origin. The origin is at 0 on the $x - axis$ and 0 on the $y - axis$.

23) Answer: B.

All angles in every triangle add up to $180°$. Let x be the angle ABC. Then: $180 = 48 + 87 + x \Rightarrow x = 45°$

24) Answer: C.

$2.75 per mile for the first 14 miles. Therefore, the cost for the first 14 miles is:

14 × $2.75 = $38.5

$3.05 per mile for each mile over 14, therefore, 6 miles over 14 miles cost:

6 × $3.05 = $18.3

In total, David pays: $38.5 + $18.3 = $56.8

25) Answer: C.

Write a proportion and solve.

13 gallons: 546 miles ⇒ 1 gallon: 546 ÷ 13 = 42 miles

26) Answer: A.

The students that had to go to summer school is 7 out of $49 = \frac{7}{49} = \frac{1}{7}$

Therefore $\frac{6}{7}$ students did not have to go to summer school.

27) Answer: B.

6 steak dinners = 6 × $9.25 = $55.5

28) Answer: D.

4 garbage trucks can collect the trash of 28 homes. Then, one garbage truck can collect the trash of 7 homes.

To collect trash of 56 houses, 8 (56 ÷ 7) garbage trucks are required.

29) Answer: B.

6 cups: 1 hour

390 cups: 390 ÷ 6 = 65 hours

30) Answer: D.

Write a proportion and solve.

$$\frac{\frac{1}{5}}{68} = \frac{1}{x} \Rightarrow x = 68 \times 5 = 340$$

Practice Test 5

SBAC - Mathematics

Answers and Explanations

1) Answer: C.

To find the answer, subtract 64,587 from 65,632.

$65{,}632 - 64{,}587 = 1{,}045 \; miles$

2) Answer: A.

Let x be the new price after discount.

$x = 60 \times (100 - 30)\% = 60 \times 70\% = 60 \times 0.70 = 42 \Rightarrow x = \$42$

3) Answer: A.

Use area of rectangle formula.

Area of a rectangle $= width \times length \Rightarrow D = w \times l \Rightarrow w = \dfrac{D}{l} = \dfrac{D}{10}$

4) Answer: B.

2 eggs for 1 cake. Therefore, 180 eggs can be used for $(180 \div 2)$ 90 cakes.

5) Answer: D.

To list the fractions from least to greatest, you can convert the fractions to decimal.

$\dfrac{3}{7} = 0.43; \dfrac{2}{3} = 0.67; \dfrac{4}{10} = 0.4; \dfrac{1}{8} = 0.125; \dfrac{5}{13} = 0.38$

$\dfrac{1}{8} = 0.125, \dfrac{5}{13} = 0.38, \dfrac{4}{10} = 0.4, \dfrac{3}{7} = 0.43, \dfrac{2}{3} = 0.67$

Option D shows the fractions in order from least to greatest.

6) Answer: B.

4 multiplied by $\dfrac{5}{3} = \dfrac{20}{3} = 6.66$, therefore, only choice B is correct.

7) Answer: D.

To find the selling price, multiply the price by (100% – rate of discount).

Then: (190) (100% – 5%) = (190) (0.95) = 180.5

8) Answer: D.

An acute angle is any angle smaller than 90 degrees.

From the options provided, only D (30 degrees) is smaller than 90.

9) Answer: C.

Plug in 40 for A in the equations. Only option A works.

$A \times 40 = 400$

$10 \times 40 = 400$

10) Answer: B.

First, find the missing side of the trapezoid. The perimeter of the trapezoid below is 100.

Therefore, the missing side of the trapezoid (its height) is:

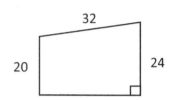

$100 - 20 - 32 - 24 = 100 - 76 = 24$

Area of a trapezoid: $A = \frac{1}{2} h (b1 + b2)$

$= \frac{1}{2} (24) (20 + 24) = 528$

11) Answer: A.

There are 90 cards in the bag and 10 of them are white. Then, 10 out of 90 cards are white. You can write this as: $\frac{10}{90}$. To simplify this fraction, divide both numerator and denominator by 10. Then: $\frac{10}{90} = \frac{1}{9}$

12) Answer: C.

1 meter of the rope = 700 grams

5.5 meter of the rope = $5.5 \times 700 = 3{,}850$ grams = 3.85 kilograms

13) Answer: D.

Lily eats 2 pancakes in 1 minute $\Rightarrow$ Lily eats 2×8 pancakes in 8 minutes (16).

Ella eats $2\frac{1}{4}$ pancakes in 1 minute $\Rightarrow$ Ella eats $2\frac{1}{4} \times 8$ pancakes in 8 minutes ($\frac{72}{4} = 18$).

In total Lily and Ella eat 16 + 18=34 pancakes in 8 minutes.

14) Answer: B.

To solve this problem, divide $3\frac{3}{4}$ by $\frac{1}{8}$.

$3\frac{3}{4} \div \frac{1}{8} = \frac{15}{4} \div \frac{1}{8} = \frac{15}{4} \times \frac{8}{1} = 30$

15) Answer: D.

The question is that number $732,636.7$ is how many times of number 7.326367. The answer is $100,000$.

16) Answer: D.

Use volume of cube formula.

Volume= $length \times width \times height \Rightarrow V = 5 \times 4 \times 10 \Rightarrow V = 200 \ cm^3$

17) Answer: C.

Use percent formula: $\text{part} = \frac{\text{percent}}{100} \times \text{whole}$

$50 = \frac{\text{percent}}{100} \times 80 \Rightarrow 50 = \frac{\text{percent} \times 80}{100} \Rightarrow 50 = \frac{\text{percent} \times 8}{10}$, multiply both sides by 10.

$500 = \text{percent} \times 8$, divide both sides by $8 \Rightarrow 62.5 = \text{percent}$

18) Answer: B.

Use area and circumference of circle formula.

Area of a circle $= \pi r^2 \Rightarrow 144\pi = \pi r^2 \Rightarrow r = 12$

Circumference of a circle $= 2\pi r \Rightarrow C = 2 \times 12 \times \pi \Rightarrow C = 24\pi$

19) Answer: B.

Alice drives 76 miles in one hour. Therefore, she drives 1,900 miles in about ($1,900 \div 76$) 25 hours.

20) Answer: C.

5 yards $= 5 \times 36 = 180$ inches, 4 feet $= 4 \times 12 = 48$ inches

5 yards 4 feet and 12 inches $= 180$ inches $+ 48$ inches $+ 12$ inches $= 240$ inches

21) Answer: A.

Simplify each option provided using order of operations rules.

A. $10 - (-5) + (-27) = 15 - 27 = -12$

B. $4 + (-5) \times (-4) = 4 + 20 = 24$

C. $-2 \times (-2) + (-5) \times (-11) = 4 + 55 = 59$

D. $(-3) \times (-8) + 5 = 24 + 5 = 29$

Only option A is -12.

22) Answer: A.

$$\frac{7}{9} \times \frac{3}{7} = \frac{7 \times 3}{9 \times 7} = \frac{21}{63} = \frac{1}{3}$$

23) Answer: B.

Use area of rectangle formula.

Area= $length \times width \Rightarrow A = \frac{4}{9} \times \frac{3}{16} \Rightarrow A = \frac{1}{12}$ inches

24) Answer: C.

ABC Corporation's income $= \frac{5}{2}$ management's predicted income.

$\$250,000 = \frac{5}{2}$ management's predicted income

management's predicted income $= \$250,000 \times \frac{2}{5} = \$100,000$

25) Answer: D.

Find the area of the room which is a square. Use area of square formula.

$S = a^2 \Rightarrow S = 20\ feet \times 20\ feet = 400$ square feet

26) Answer: C.

$$\frac{1}{2} + \frac{8}{15} - \frac{1}{30} = \frac{(15 \times 1) + (2 \times 8) - (1 \times 1)}{30} = \frac{30}{30} = 1$$

27) Answer: D.

Use percent formula: part $= \frac{percent}{100} \times$ whole

$800 = \frac{percent}{100} \times 4,000 \Rightarrow 800 =$ percent $\times 40 \Rightarrow$ percent $= 20$

28) Answer: A.

Use area of rectangle formula. $A = a \times b \Rightarrow A = 64 \times 30 \Rightarrow A = 1,920$

Divide the area by 16 ($4 \times 4 = 16$ squares) to find the number of squares needed.

$1,920 \div 16 = 120$

29) Answer: D.

Write the numbers in order: 4, 4, 6, 9, 10, 11, 13

Median is the number in the middle. Therefore, the median is 9.

30) Answer: B.

Use PEMDAS (order of operation): $18 + [4 \times 3] \div 3 = 18 + (12) \div 3 = 18 + (12 \div 3) = 22$

Practice Test 6

SBAC - Mathematics

Answers and Explanations

1) Answer: C.

$6 + (10 \times 24) = 6 + 240 = 246$

2) Answer: D.

1 hour: $5.5

8 hours: $8 \times \$5.5 = \$44$

3) Answer: B.

$10 - 5\frac{1}{3} = \frac{30}{3} - \frac{16}{3} = \frac{14}{3}$

4) Answer: D.

The number of guests that are not present are: $(240 - 210)$ 30 out of $240 = \frac{30}{240}$

Change the fraction to percent: $\frac{30}{240} \times 100\% = 12.5\%$

5) Answer: A.

Each kilogram is 1,000 grams. 23,032 grams $= \frac{23,032}{1,000} = 23.032$ kilograms. Therefore, 23,032 grams are greater than the 23.023 kg.

6) Answer: B.

Aria teaches 36 hours for three identical courses. Therefore, she teaches 6 hours for each course. Aria earns $25 per hour. Therefore, she earned $150 ($6 \times 25$) for each course.

7) Answer: C.

The number of female students in the class is: $(60 - 40)$ 20 out of $60 = \frac{20}{60}$

Change the fraction to percent: $\frac{20}{60} \times 100\% = 33.3\%$

8) Answer: C.

Write a proportion and solve.

$\frac{10 \text{ soft drinks}}{18 \text{ guests}} = \frac{x}{153 \text{ guests}} \Rightarrow x = \frac{153 \times 10}{18} \Rightarrow x = 85$

9) Answer: A.

$$\text{average (mean)} = \frac{\text{sum of terms}}{\text{number of terms}} \Rightarrow \text{average} = \frac{2+4+21+27+28+33+31+30}{8} \Rightarrow \text{average} = 22$$

10) Answer: B.

Every 60 minutes Emma checks her email.

In 6 hours (360 minutes), Emma checks her email ($360 \div 60$) 6 times.

11) Answer: C.

There are 70 students in the class. 49 of the are male and 21 of them are female. 21 out of 70 are female. Then:

$$\frac{21}{70} = \frac{x}{100} \rightarrow 2,100 = 70x \rightarrow x = 21,00 \div 70 = 30\%$$

12) Answer: D.

Divide the number flowers by 15: $735 \div 15 = 49$

13) Answer: B.

Rounding decimals is similar to rounding other numbers. If the hundredths and thousandths places of a decimal is forty-nine or less, they are dropped, and the tenths place does not change. For example, rounding 0.843 to the nearest tenth would give 0.8. Therefore, 9,258.48991 rounded to the nearest tenth is 9,258.5.

14) Answer: D.

Perimeter of rectangle formula:

$$P = 2\,(length + width) \Rightarrow 134 = 2\,(l + 37) \Rightarrow l = 30$$

Area of rectangle formula: $A = length \times width \Rightarrow A = 30 \times 37 \Rightarrow A = 1,110$

15) Answer: D.

Use volume of rectangle prism formula.

$$V = length \times width \times height \Rightarrow V = 11 \times 3 \times 9 \Rightarrow V = 297$$

16) Answer: B.

The diameter of the circle is 12 inches. Therefore, the radius of the circle is 6 inches.

Use circumference of circle formula. $C = 2\pi r \Rightarrow C = 2 \times 3.14 \times 6 \Rightarrow C = 37.68$

17) Answer: A.

The line segment is from 5 to -5. Therefore, the line is 10 units.

$$5 - (-5) = 5 + 5 = 10$$

18) Answer: B.

Plug in $x = -4$ in each equation.

A. $x(4x - 5) = 75 \rightarrow (-4)(4(-4) - 5) = (-4) \times (-16 - 4) = 80$

B. $4(6 - x) = 40 \rightarrow 4(6 - (-4) = 4(10) = 40$

C. $3(2x + 5) = 12 \rightarrow 3(2(-4) + 5) = 3(-8 + 5) = -9$

D. $4x - 6 = -20 \rightarrow 4(-4) - 6 = -16 - 6 = -12$

Only option B.

19) Answer: A.

Peter's speed $= \dfrac{200}{5} = 40$

Jason's speed $= \dfrac{210}{7} = 30$

$\dfrac{The\ average\ speed\ of\ peter}{The\ average\ speed\ of\ Jason} = \dfrac{40}{30}$ equals to: $\dfrac{4}{3}$ or $4 : 3$

20) Answer: B.

4 workers can walk 8 dogs $\Rightarrow$ 1 workers can walk 2 dogs.

9 workers can walk (9×2) 18 dogs.

21) Answer: D.

In fractions, when denominators increase, the value of fractions decrease and as much as numerators increase, the value of fractions increase. Therefore, the least one of this list is: $\dfrac{1}{9}$ and the greatest one of this list is: $\dfrac{1}{2}$

22) Answer: C.

The horizontal axis in the coordinate plane is called the $x - axis$. The vertical axis is called the $y - axis$. The point at which the two axes intersect is called the origin. The origin is at 0 on the $x - axis$ and 0 on the $y - axis$.

23) Answer: B.

All angles in every triangle add up to $180°$. Let x be the angle ABC. Then: $180 = 45 + 90 + x \Rightarrow x = 45°$

24) Answer: C.

$3.25 per mile for the first 25 miles. Therefore, the cost for the first 20 miles is:

$25 \times \$3.25 = \$81.25$

$4.06 per mile for each mile over 25, therefore, 5 miles over 25 miles cost:

$5 \times \$4.06 = \$20.3$

In total, David pays: $\$81.25 + \$20.3 = \$101.55$

25) Answer: C.

Write a proportion and solve.

19 gallons: 608 miles $\Rightarrow$ 1gallon: $608 \div 19 = 32$ miles

26) Answer: A.

The students that had to go to summer school is 6 out of $24 = \frac{6}{24} = \frac{1}{4}$

Therefore $\frac{3}{4}$ students did not have to go to summer school.

27) Answer: B.

3 steak dinners = $3 \times \$7.75 = \$23.25$

28) Answer: D.

6 garbage trucks can collect the trash of 48 homes. Then, one garbage truck can collect the trash of 8 homes.

To collect trash of 72 houses, 9 ($72 \div 8$) garbage trucks are required.

29) Answer: B.

9 cups: 1 hour

783 cups: $783 \div 9 = 87$ hours

30) Answer: D.

Write a proportion and solve.

$\frac{\frac{1}{6}}{80} = \frac{1}{x} \Rightarrow x = 80 \times 6 = 480$

"End"

Made in the USA
Las Vegas, NV
15 April 2024

88734764R00063